A
PSYCHIC
DISCOVERS JESUS

Tim Thompson

A Psychic Discovers Jesus
ISBN: 978-0-88144-525-1
Copyright © 2010 by Tim Thompson

Contents

Foreword

I recommend this book for inspection by every pastor or person who feels called to enter the ministry. It gives just the kind of information that every minister needs in order to understand how he/ she may come across to the new believer who is sincerely looking for a church home.

We say that we preach a Gospel that will save from the uttermost-to-the-guttermost, yet when confronted with those who have truly come from the depths of sin, too many pastors readily give up on trying to shepherd these souls for whom Christ died. Worse still, they may respond from their carnal backgrounds and even drive them away, in some cases even heaping abuse on those who are truly seeking help and a place to belong in the Body of Christ.

It is high time that the Church of the 21st Century stop resembling a defensive holding action against the onslaught of Satan, and start resembling more the power-packed Primitive Church which was described by the Apostle Paul in 1 Corinthians 6:9-11:

> *Know ye not that the unrighteous shall not inherit the kingdom of God? Be not deceived: neither fornicators, nor idolaters, nor adulterers, nor effeminate, nor abusers of themselves with mankind,*

nor thieves, nor covetous, nor drunkards, nor revilers, nor extortioners, shall inherit the kingdom of God.

And such were some of you: but ye are washed, but ye are sanctified, but ye are justified in the name of the Lord Jesus, and by the Spirit of our God.

Tim's enthusiasm and fiery determination to win others to Christ, a refreshing characteristic particularly manifested in new converts, should encourage and inspire every minister to seek new converts more actively than ever to revitalize and further energize their churches. The thing that helped him persist in his faith in Christ during his own years in the wilderness without the direct loving support of the Church was God's promise to him personally that if he would remain teachable, faithful, and accountable, he would be able to fulfilling his calling.

I believe Tim has reached that place of green pastures and still waters spoken of in the 23rd Psalm. I believe he will be greatly used of God as he begins his ministry in earnest. I think this book is timely and perfect suited for the hour in which we are living. May God bless you is my prayer.

Dr. Dean Helland,
Doctor of Ministry from Oral Roberts University
Missionary, Pastor, Evangelist, Counselor, Educator

Dedication

First and foremost, I would to dedicate this book to Jesus Christ. I really mean that, because when I was the worst possible condition a person could be in spiritually, mentally, emotionally and physically, Jesus came down with all His glory and rescued me in the pit of hell I was in.

My body was extremely ill, I was losing my mind, and I was on the path to everlasting damnation, but through God's mercy, grace, compassion and love, He rescued me. Even though this book is about my personal experiences, it is really just another chapter about the glory, compassion, love, mercy, grace and power of Jesus Christ. There's nothing I can compare Christ to.

I was in the midst of complete darkness and seeking after all forms of darkness. Every imaginable sin was in my life in abundance, but when I cried out to Jesus Christ, he heard my cry for help. So may all credit for the transformation of my life from the kingdom of darkness to the Kingdom of Light must be given to Jesus Christ, the Son of the most high God.

Also I want to dedicate this book to Dr. Dean Helland, because though his life followed quite different paths than my own, he has given me so much of his time just listening to me, opening his heart with compassion and love. For years I was rejected by so many pastors I had approached because of my past, but I knew that wasn't the way it was supposed to be, and for a long time, Satan kept trying to get me to be bitter toward Christians, but I knew some day i would find love in the Church, so I kept believing that I would find the spiritual father I was yearning for. God has blessed me may times over with the spiritual relationship I have been able to develop with Dr. Helland. All my life I just wanted to be heard, accepted and loved. I have found these in my friend and mentor, Dr.Helland.

With his help, my family and I have finally found a church that is reaching out to those who too often have been avoided, even rejected by the normal church-goers. I thank God for the many friends and great encouragement we have found as we have bonded with this godly church that is actively reaching out for the lost wherever and however it can.

I would also like to thank my loving wife and best friend for standing by me through the years and believing in us.

Acknowledgements

I would personally like to thank all those who have given their time, love, support, along with those hundreds of emails and countless phone conversations.

To my loving wife, who has walked with me through countless battles and has endured great hardships with me, but has witnessed God's grace, mercy, compassion, blessings and love break forth in our lives.

To Dr.Dean Helland, for being my mentor, my loving spiritual father, my dear friend, and the editor of this book, for his numerous phone conversations, scores of email communications, lunches together, and for allowing me to be myself, for your support, patience, kindness, compassion, long periods of just listening. Above all, Dr. Dean, thank you for your genuine love and your acceptance of me, because not once did you ever look down on me for opening up to you. I can't express the gratitude I have towards God for you.

To my parents, for not giving up on me after I had attempted suicide and was put in the hospital for being homicidal.

To Ray, for countless phone conversations and many hours spent on the phone with me. Thanks for being there for me!

To Chris, the best teacher I have ever had in any class I have ever taken. Thank you for giving me the privilege of being your friend, and thank you for answering the many emails I have sent you. Thanks for all your support and genuine love. You didn't reject me, no matter how much I opened up my past to you.

And to Jeremy, thanks so much for your patience and help with the computer. I so admire the way you have taught me so much about computers, about accepting people just as they are, and listening to me pour out things that were not pleasant to hear. Thank you for not rejecting me and never looking down on me for my ignorance of so many things. Thank you! And most of all, your forgiveness has meant more than I can ever tell.

A Short Version of My Testimony

By Tim Thompson

Back when I was six-years-old, my brother and I were walking on a frozen lake thinking that we were in a park when the ice gave way. I fell in and my brother grabbed me, and then he fell in, too. While I was saved by him, no one was able to save him, and three days later I woke up out of a coma and my hell began.

At my brother's funeral, the priest said that the good Lord needed him, so he took him. Well, I didn't know how to deal with so much pain, and after two weeks, I couldn't handle my brother being gone, so I decided to go where he was and that means death.

So one day in my closet, filled with hatred towards God for taking my brother, I pulled a blanket up to my chest and pretended to be dead. I found a lot of joy and peace in this, but after the second or third time that I did that, I heard a voice that mocked God. It made me feel really good to know that I wasn't the only one that hated God. Within a short time, I heard such mocking and such hatred toward God that I just felt like whoever this is really understands me.

So I just kept getting into my pretend coffin more and more. Then one day I heard a voice say, "I love you, and I care a lot about you. God is ruthless and doesn't care about you." So at the age of six, my hatred of God increased a lot. Then I started developing severe nightmares, and my parents were getting frustrated with me, so they suggested I see a priest. But my spirit friend said, "I will give you words to say, so don't be afraid." It was right. The priest did not know how to help me.

Then one day at age seven, I went into the spirit world and had my first demonic vision. I saw myself putting an axe in my dad's skull. But my spirit friend said, "Don't tell anyone, because if you do, you will be locked up forever." I then knew my friend was real, because I could hear him crystal clear. About a year later, I now had several spirit friends, and most of them I could see. But Raw was a spirit friend that scared other spirit friends, because his name was "war" spelled backwards.

Then I started drinking a little bit here and there, and that really caused my friends to be more active. By age twelve, I decided to hate all people of color. It seemed fun, and all my spirit friends really liked it. See, I wanted to please them, because the more I pleased them, the more they would say, "We love you and care about you."

By age fifteen, my severe nightmares stopped, because I became friends with a spirit called Nightmare, but my other playmate spirits were more loving. By sixteen, most friends of mine from school wanted to look at pornography, so I just pretended to like it, too, this but actually I was thinking about how to kill people. I considered Ted Bundy and Hitler to be very genuine men, and I knew both of them were controlled by spirits.

I was introduced to the Ouija board at seventeen, and my friend said it was boring, but I heard it growl at me, and this really turned me on. So I quit being into racism, and I dived into occultism. By age eighteen, I began developing a really bad habit of taking cocaine and meth, but my spirit friends let me know that from my childhood, God had been my problem, and I was to hate those that followed Him.

Well, I had gotten heavy into cursing people and things as a child, so I now began seeing things happen to those I cursed, like people getting hurt when I spoke evil against them. At age twenty,

I got heavy in to Satanism. I told a social worker that I am going to commit murder with a sledgehammer. At that, I was court-ordered to go in to a psychiatric ward. While in there, I was diagnosed with many different mental illnesses. But that was really funny to me, because these spirits spoke through me and confused everybody.

One day in another ward, I heard this real gentle voice say, "I love you, my child. Please call out to me." But after I heard that voice, it seemed like all hell broke loose. After getting out of another rehab, I went to a friend for help, and he took me to the wealthiest tarot card reader in the state. This woman read Tarot cards even for doctors and attorneys. But while we were in her kitchen, she called my friend into the other room and said, "What in the hell are you doing? Don't you realize the demons in him are by far more powerful than the spirits I deal with?" After that, we were ordered to leave. Well, because I was able to get the Ouija board to move around in so many ways, I started scaring all my friends.

After six rehabs and seven mental wards, I tried to commit suicide. My psychologist took his life, but I failed even at slitting my own wrist. I just gave up. I was dying, because of liver problems. I had no food and no money for medications because I had the flu. So I knelt down at my bed and asked God to kill me or show me some type of happiness. When I did that, Jesus Christ himself came down through the ceiling and said to me, "You are set free from all your drug and alcohol addiction. You will no longer need your antidepressants. You are going to do great and mighty things for my kingdom." Well, it was so. I was completely delivered instantly.

Since then, I have traveled to six states and bought a lot of books, tapes, CD's, and talked to a lot of people with no one helping me, but a facing lot of rejection. People told me that if I were really saved, I would not be having any more psychic problems. That went on for some twenty years. However, I kept on believing that one day I would find freedom and would be blessed with a real spiritual dad.

That finally happened recently with Dr. Dean Helland. He was able to accept me and love me just the way I am. After meeting him, I took an intense course called Men of Destiny. It taught me the steps to freedom. Chris was one of its teachers. There, I was allowed just to be free to speak about all the hurt that many Christians, including pastors, have done to me since I got saved. I can now say that I am finally free. Yes, I have real freedom! My true test was in the fourth weekend of the Destiny class.

That week I called Ray, my other mentor, and told him that a woman had appeared to me in a vision saying, "Please contact my children and husband and let them know I'm okay." She was very beautiful, but her throat was slit. She said, "I was snowmobiling in Minnesota with my husband and friends, and I ran right in to a barbwire fence. The next thing I knew, I woke up in a steel metal box like a refrigerator."

Well, I called Ray, and he said not to contact her family at all, because this is very demonic. I told Ray the city and state where she was killed and all her family members' names. Later, Dr. Dean showed me from the scriptures just how demonic this was, and I was able to turn away from it and rebuke it and see it leave my life.

I believe everybody would benefit from that Destiny class because my prison walls, which no one could see, fell down there, and I am walking on with Christ. My bondage that had no chains was really there, but not now. Praise God! Praise God I'm free!

CHAPTER 1

From Hopelessness to More Hopelessness

I came from an all-American upper-class family. My parents were pretty happy generally until a tragedy took place with my brother. When I was very young, my brother and I were involved in a horrible drowning accident. My brother managed to save my life, but then he drowned, because there was no one there to save him.

I remember that at his funeral, the Catholic priest said that the Good Lord needed him so much that He took him. From that point on, I began to hate and resent God deeply. I missed my brother so much. He was my closest friend and playmate. I was so about confused about why a God that is supposed to be loving should want to hurt me and my family so much. Nobody wanted to talk about it, but I could not understand why my brother had died when it had my idea to go swimming.

Then one day about two weeks after his death, I just wanted to hear him and have someone to play with, so I decided to go where he was. I laid down in my closet put a blanket over my chest and began to cry. I thought that if I could pretend to be dead, I might find him. Well, for the first time since his death, I felt like I was there with him.

I started talking to my dead brother on a regular basis going into my pretend coffin. At first I only did this once a week for about twenty minutes at a time, but as time went on, I started going into my pretend coffin daily, sometimes for up to an hour. I thought, "Wow, I am really communicating with my dead brother. As time went on, I began hearing my brother talk to me and we would play together throughout the day.

After that, I started having severe nightmares, and my parents didn't know what to do, so they had me see a priest. Since most Catholics don't understand spiritual warfare, that did not seem to do me any good. As time went on, I started having nightmares all the time, and I could see my parent's frustration at this. But I kept hearing a voice say, "If you tell anyone about us, they will think you're crazy, and they will lock you up." So I decided not to tell anyone what I was going through, because I felt abandoned by my brother and that God had rejected me. I felt hopeless.

Then one night I had a very bizarre dream. I dreamt that a silver cord was connected to me, and I left my body and was having a great time, but the thought came to me that if I would fly out of the window and someone should happen to shut it, I would be lost out there for good. After that night, I started having out-of-the-body experiences, and my nightmares stopped. I realized that if I would become friends with all these spiritual beings I was seeing, they would not hurt me or scare me anymore.

What I have learned through the years since then is that when it comes to seducing spirits, the sexual aspect of seducing spirits that so many teach about is just a small part of it. In every way possible, these spirits want you to come against God's authority and God's righteous judgments. So their purpose is to drive you away from God with empty promises and lies. So even though many of my spirit friends were very evil looking, I just started to talk to all of them. I did not realize until I got saved that these were actually demons.

I can remember so well one night meditating on dying in a car accident. During that time, I saw many of my spirit friends around me mocking and ridiculing God. So I felt comfort, knowing that someone could feel my pain and understand my severe hatred toward God. But as time went on, I couldn't understand why these spirit friends of mine hated God so much. At times I would feel one being come to me that was very gentle, and it would say, "God loves you." But when it would say "God loves you", I would get really confused, because I hated God, so I rejected all of what it said. As time went on, I had more visions and more thoughts of wanting to die and kill people in the process, just for fun.

Then one day I had my incredible vision that made a deep impression on me. I saw myself bury an axe in my dad's skull. From that point on, I was certain that this was really real, and my spirit friends were real, too, though in a different dimension than the reality we know in the tangible world. I so desperately wanted to tell someone, but this powerful spirit of fear would torment me by saying, "If you say anything, they will lock you up forever."

So I would seek my dead brother's advice. Pretty soon I realized I was meditating so much on being killed in so many different ways that I couldn't stop thinking about it. After that night, I started feeling unworthy to be loved and lost all hope of ever being loved. So I just pretty much gave up all together. I went to look for others who believed that what I was experiencing was real. Those that were in the occult and wanting to find out more about the occult became my closest friends.

One day a friend of mine introduced me to a man who was very well known for writing hate literature and exaggerated lies so people would not believe much in God. He said, "I asked you to come into my home because you have a strong gift of leadership, and I want your help to raise up a powerful teen group to help spread the word that we must protect our Aryan rights."

I felt honored knowing that he saw something good in me, but I just wanted to find out more about the unseen world. Well, by expressing this, I found myself turning to Satanism. Devastated that the psychologist that I was seeing at the time took his life and also by the fact that some of my dearest friends were also committing suicide, all I saw was more hopelessness. So I thought, "There has to be a reason that I am alive." So I sought out more evil and more of what Satanism was all about. Soon I found myself around people who were also hopeless and full of despair.

By all appearances, they seemed to have it all; drugs, parties, plenty of sex, etc., but I was seeking answers about why was I here alive on the earth. Then one day at my job, these two guys were talking about God's goodness, and how many people don't see it. Well, I got interested in what they were saying, so I asked one of the guys, "Do you really believe what you're saying?" He was so shocked he said, "You have got to meet my pastor." So I agreed and we met at a coffee shop. I told the pastor, "I see a lot of hopelessness and I don't see any point to life, so suicide seems a way out."

The pastor really surprised me when he responded by saying, "Since you see suicide as your only way out, why don't you go ahead and take your own life?"

Well, since he didn't invite me to church or talk to me about Jesus, I figured, "Well, he doesn't know who Jesus is either." So I figured that since no one had any answers, I should just find ways to please myself and no one else. As a result, I became very hardened towards Christians and anyone who was on TV talking about God. I made it a point to hate everything that was of God. But by doing this, I started being eaten alive by depression and loneliness. I had plenty of friends, but I was dying of loneliness.

So I had a plan--to drink myself to death. But when I developed liver and kidney problems, I decided that it wasn't any fun waking up on a hospital bed time after time. It hit me hard that my so-called good friends didn't come see me in the hospital, either. But then, as I look back, they didn't come see me at the rehabs either. But I figured that if a pastor agrees with my spirit friend that life is meaningless, who does have answers?

One day I called a friend who I thought could help me and who was big into séances. He said, "You just have to meet a friend of mine that makes a good living reading the cards." I found that Tarot card-readers fascinated me because they liked the spirit world just as much as I did, and they didn't like reality much either. So I got my friend to take me over to meet her, and I was really excited. But what happened next left really bowled me over!

As we were waiting for her to come out of the waiting room and meet us, she called my friend into the next room and said, "Get that guy out of my house! What in hell are you trying to do to me?" He just stood there and said, "What is going on?" And I heard her say, "That guy has more powerful spirits around him than I have around me, and they will kill me or destroy me if I mess up."

She kept on yelling at my friend to get me out of her house. My friend after that moment was never the same. He kept saying to me, "Who are you?" and "What's going on with you? She has read cards for years, and I have never seen her so terrified."

For the first time in my whole life there was a war inside of me like never before. I just couldn't let it go. Did I possess powers that this Tarot card reader couldn't handle? Or, was there really a God out there that did have greater power than the devil, and He wanted me to get to know Him? That was when the battle inside me really began to get much worse.

All of a sudden I felt like, "Wow! There must be more to life than what everyone is telling me!" That Tarot-card-reader made a lot of money and was very successful at what she did, so what is it that she saw? I didn't ever find out what made this woman so nervous, because my friend didn't want to be around me again after that. Years later I found out that people who dabble deep into the occult can actually see not only demons, but they see an aurora about God's people who are really serving God. So now I was on my search again for answers.

I contacted people who I knew dabbled a lot with the Ouija board, but most of them didn't want to be around me either. I finally found someone that would talk to me, but he let me know he wasn't happy about it. As we began to become friends, he also suddenly quit and said he never wanted to be around me again he got so scared. I didn't know what to do. But then one day, I got a call from some of my friends who said it was getting too intense, and they were quitting everything in the occult, because it wasn't just for fun any longer. It was getting out of control. Then one by one, the very people that I had wanted to look to for answers started getting killed in car accidents or committed suicide.

Some people who got really scared of the occult decided to try it one more time, then ended up killing themselves. Such deep despair and loneliness were setting in that I tried to end my life with cocaine. But once again, I heard this small still voice saying, "I love you and I am here for you." But this time it was different, because it deeply touched my life to the point where I felt like crying. After that, a spirit friend came to me and said, "God can't love you. You have done too many evil things." So I started condemning myself all the time.

Then one day I met this girl that I liked, and we started living together. She said, "Will you go to church with me sometime? I thought, "Why not?", because I wanted some answers to life. Well, I met with the pastor on Wednesday night after hearing him preach on Sunday, but it was a disaster. I opened up to him, and he got so bound by fear after I told him what had been going on in my life that he said, "You will bring major attacks on this church and we can't have you do that, so I would suggest you seek help somewhere else."

Well, after that I decided to give up on God and Jesus, so on Friday night I met a woman who dabbled a lot in Black Magic. She was fun to be around, and we became pretty good friends. One day she called me and said, "The spirits are telling me you're a powerful medium." So she had me hold objects, and I could tell her where they came from. I was so excited I thought, "Wow! Now I know what I am supposed to do, and I enjoy this." But as I got deeper into it, I felt as if something or someone was controlling me.

Soon she contacted a crystal ball reader, and they were amazed at how accurate I was. I was told that I could make a good living off this, but soon it was no longer me doing it. I realized that there was something overpowering me and doing it through me. Pretty soon I met more people that knew me as a "psychic", and I enjoyed that title until one night when I was reading things about trying to connect with the dead. I was lying in bed and felt this woman-like figure come to me, and we had a sexual tryst. That hit me hard, because no one had ever told me that anything like that would happen.

I told my friend about it, and she introduced me to a witch who was in her late sixties. This lady told me, "Soon you will learn to turn your whole mind, body and spirit over to these spirits, and they will make you a good living." This witch told me that most of who she was, was a spirit. After that I thought, "Wow! Just how deep can all this go?"

In time I learned that many people I was now meeting with had a spirit guide. Their spirit guide actually became a part of their identity. So I decided that since I was gaining many new friends again, I should seek out this gift of being a psychic, even though it meant losing my very self. By all appearances, I seemed to have it all, but on the inside, I wasn't sure who I was anymore. And I could tell I was losing my mind. I knew I was in hell in my mind, because I wondered, "What if I lose my mind?" I didn't know yet what the Bible says about that in Isaiah 44:25, that God makes diviners lose their minds and go mad.

My Conversion

But God is real, and He really does care. However, I kept thinking of all of God's so-called people who had rejected me and showed me no love or genuine concern. I ended up in the hospital with a severe liver infection, and my kidneys were in really bad shape by now because of consuming all that alcohol. I got out of the hospital and got the flu. My apartment had no heat, because I had forgotten to pay the bill. I had no food and no medication, so it was a hopeless situation all around. For the first time, I felt my body was really dying, and I was too weak to do anything. So I just gave up. I figured this was it. My end had finally come.

Around midnight I got down on my knees beside the bed and asked God to kill me or show me some type of happiness. To my surprise, I suddenly saw Jesus come down through the ceiling. He was as white as snow. He had the figure of a man, and said, "From this day forward, I will take your alcohol addiction away and your addiction to drugs. You will no longer need anti-depressant pills either, because I am going to give you a new life and a new hope. You will come to know me and know my love for you. I will teach you many things, and you will do mighty things for my kingdom."

The next day I woke up and was completely healed. So I called my friend who is a social worker, and he said, "Let's test your mind to see what's going on." I had told him what had happened the night before. He tested me and said, "I haven't ever seen anyone healed like this before, so call your doctor, and tell him you need your liver and kidneys tested right away. and let me know the results." My doctor tested my liver and kidneys and said, "This is impossible! Your body is healed!"

When I got the news, I was so amazed that all I could do was thank God all day long. In Luke 8:44, it says Jesus came to heal the brokenhearted. For the first time in many years, I had peace, joy beyond understanding, and I was consumed with the presence of feeling loved without having to do anything to deserve it. Jesus Christ had come into my apartment that was filled with wickedness and rescued me! A nobody became a somebody! I had done almost anything one can imagine just to find acceptance. Almost every wicked and foul spirit had been invited into this apartment where many occult things had taken place!

To just give you, the reader, an idea of how evil it was when I had friends over, we would have a contest to see who could draw the most satanic crosses when we got bored. Spirits of confusion, despair, suicide, rejection, hopelessness, and depression were not rejected but welcomed in. But because of what had just happened to me, I just couldn't stop praising God for saving a wretched man like me!

Every time I think about this, it just amazes me, because most people I know can't fathom some of the things I have done. You see, if Jesus loved me that much to go into a place that was that full of evil to rescue me, just imagine where He will go for you. Jesus didn't come to condemn the world but to save it. Too many people get confused about Jesus and religion.

Jesus loves us, and like it says in 1 John 3:8, Jesus came to destroy the works of the devil. I love sharing this with people, because, like it says in Luke 7:47, those who have been forgiven much will love much. Nothing I can ever say will be good enough to say "thank you for saving a horrible sinner like me." No matter how many sins we may have committed, it will never compare to what He has done for me. I have committed such unthinkable sins, but, praise God, my sins have all been washed away by the blood of Jesus Christ.

Now I can walk in freedom because of what Christ's blood has done for me. I am forgiven of all those things and God, through His mercy, doesn't see any of my past at all. What an awesome God He really is! No matter what sins we may have committed, God can and will forgive us if we will just humbly go to Him with a repentant heart. Jesus loves for us far more than we can ever know. Hebrews 4:15-16 points out that Jesus Christ can empathize with our weaknesses, so even if we feel like there is no hope, there is always hope in Christ Jesus.

According to the Word of God, we become a new creation in Christ after we get saved. Even if we do not hear a voice from God, we need to maintain our eyes and heart focused on Him. Just because just because He is not speaking to us when we want him to doesn't mean he doesn't care or that he's not listening. He is asking us to press through in prayer even more to seek his face.

Many generations back, a great man of God who was deeply respected and honored ran into this very same problem, but it cost him his life. King Saul, since fear had gripped his heart and he didn't get a word from God, decided that he would seek out a medium which in today's life is also called a psychic. It's a very fascinating story and is found in 1 Samuel 28:6-25, and its consequences are explained in 1 Chronicles 10:13-14. We, as Christians, need to realize that there is no other way to God than through Jesus Christ. The story is really sad in so many ways, because even when a seducing spirit makes it seem like there's something out there better than God Almighty, we must remember that though at the moment it might look good, later on, it could cost us everything.

CHAPTER 2

Demonic
Attacks Exposed

I moved away from that city and started up a whole new life. I met some really nice Christian guys one day, and they let me know they were going to the university there, and they asked me to check out their church. So I met their pastor, and he wanted to know how I got saved. I let him know about what had happened to me, and how I got transformed. Well, his face about fell off, and I wasn't really liked from that point on. He became cold towards me and the assistant pastor told me I might like a church somewhere else.

So one day as I was at work making my deliveries, because I was a delivery driver, I saw a small café and it looked cool, so I went in. They were selling Bible tracts there, so I bought some. That is when I met Pastor Ted. He was a young pastor, but really excited about God, so he invited me to his church. I will never forget how much faith this man had. As time went on, we became close, so I started to share my past with him, and he just kept loving me. He spent a lot of time teaching me about spiritual warfare and I enjoyed that a lot. But Ted, not understanding my past, only my just getting saved, prayed for me a lot. He could see the war in me was raging and that I didn't know what to do.

I know now about soul ties, which I didn't know back then, because I was losing the battle I found myself in. After about a year, a girl called me that I knew was a Christian. She asked me to move in with her, so I told Ted I was moving on, and I went back to what I had just left. I said good-bye to Ted. I thought she might help me but it was a horrible thing, ending up moving in with her. I got to know her really well, and I said "I thought you loved God". She said "I do, but Jesus is not the Son of God. He hasn't come yet."

Well, right then and there, I knew I had been fooled by thinking that this woman really wanted to live for Jesus Christ. Since I was being intimate with her, I knew we should marry, but I knew that wasn't right either, so about two weeks before the wedding, I broke off the engagement. I knew I couldn't go back to my old lifestyle, and I wasn't sure what to do. Then all of a sudden, I got a really good job.

Without my realizing it, I had been living for myself and not for Jesus Christ. By all appearances things looked great, but on the inside I was filled with turmoil again. I knew I should seek after God, but how? I kept asking myself, "How?" Well, I was being beaten up by the devil daily for about a year and a half, not knowing what to do. Then one day I got a call from a temporary agency that asked me if I would like to help them out for three days making good money. I agreed and went to work for them, and things seemed to be going well.

However, after being on the job only three hours, there was a broken water pipe I was trying to help fix, and the foreman said he would hook up a light for me to see better since I was working under a building. But when they hooked up the light for me, they forgot to check to see if the power cord was grounded. Well, it wasn't, so the electricity flowed through my body for about forty-five seconds. Since I was in about six inches of water, I got burned pretty severely internally. The doctors that treated me said about ninety percent of my right side was burned internally. I had to see doctors in three different cities because I had severe muscle spasms. Nothing was helping. My spasms kept getting worse, and I was in a lot of pain. A team of specialists decided I needed to go to the national burn center.

A good friend I had wanted to take me out, so we went on a short trip for a couple of days before I was scheduled to leave for the burn center. On the way back home, we were hit by a drunk driver. When the ambulance showed up, they could tell I had just recently been injured, so they didn't know what to do. In the ambulance, I explained what just happened to me. Anyhow, I finally ended up at the national burn center. At the burn center, I was treated for multiple problems. They said that my nervous system was badly damaged, that I would lose my ability to walk probably within a year. Then, as they ran more tests, they discovered that cancer cells were forming after my being burned, and I had a form of a cancer. The spirit of hopelessness came back over me like a flood, and I had to continually fight it. But one night, while I was sleeping, this very sinister spirit-being came into my room and I saw him. It had a head like a goat and a body like a man, but its eyes were burning hot red. He said, "I have loved you for a long time. Come and serve me, and you will be well again, and I will give you what you desire."

He showed me a lot of things that looked pleasing, but I knew in my heart that Jesus Christ died for me, and that I should serve him and him only, so I called upon the name of Jesus Christ. The next day the doctors said I was dying, but lying on that hospital bed, I had my first really big encounter with the Holy Spirit. The Holy Spirit spoke to me to the effect that I would live and not die, that the doctor was going to talk to me about how my leg was dying and that they would probably have to amputate. "But", the Lord told me, "don't believe him. I am going to heal your body to where you will be able to run again and throw a football again." So I just believed it from that moment on.

Well, just like the Holy Spirit said, the doctor told me that my leg would probably have to be amputated. As time went on, my body kept getting worse and worse, but I knew God's Holy Spirit can't lie, so I just kept believing that I would be fine. I went back to the city I was burned in and lived there for a while. Then one day the Spirit of God said, "I am going to bring you a helpmate."

I was now driving again, but the doctors told me that the cancer was slowly killing me. Well, I met this wonderful woman who did street ministry, and we became really close. We stayed pure in our relationship, fell in love, and even though I had major health problems, she eventually married me. One of my specialist said, "I need you to move to California where more specialists can see you."

So after we got married, we to California. When the doctors saw me, they said things were getting worse, but I clung to what the Spirit of God had said. I knew that when God spared my life and rescued me from drugs, he had said, "You will do mighty things for my kingdom." So I knew I was going to be healed, even though my body showed no evidence of it. My neck was getting worse now and having major spasms every day. The doctors were afraid it was going to snap. But no matter what all the specialist had to say, and no matter how much fear tried to overpower me, faith was in all my thoughts, defeating all those demonic attacks. No matter how much they talked about amputating my leg or that I would lose my ability to walk, my faith just stood solid like a rock.

I started to voice my opinion about how I knew I would be fine, but everybody thought I was in denial. The really sad part that bothered me was that everyone was just looking at how I was doing, but they had no faith at all that I would be fine. Even my pastor let me down. I could see it in his eyes and listened to his doubts, but I knew I serve a God that can heal and restore. Well, we had to move again so that I could see more specialists.

I just want to put in a quick note here. When everyone was praying for my healing, they weren't listening to the Holy Spirit. The reason I say that is because God was talking to me through this whole ordeal and showed me that He was going to have my healing manifested. He said, "Child of mine, you have been in the Word a great deal since this all started, and I am pleased with your staying in my Word. You know a lot about the enemy and how the enemy attacks, but I want you to know about me. So during this period in your life, I want you to dive in to my Word and let me carry the burden of all of your life's needs. You just stay focused on me and continually study my word daily."

You see, when I was working, I worked such long hours that I really didn't have a lot of time to study. But after getting hurt, I decided that if a normal work week is forty hours long and I had always given the enemy a large amount of time, God deserves thirty hours a week of my studying His Word or in prayer, so I did this for over a year. What many people were seeing as so bad actually turned out to be one of the greatest blessings I have ever received. That is why we should never just look at circumstances, but ask God what is going on. Too many people get depressed and confused because they are just leaning on their own understanding.

Proverbs 3:5 says, "Trust in the Lord with all your heart, and lean not on your own understanding." You see, God is asking you to trust him with your finances, life, job, career, whatever it may be. We need to quit trusting in ourselves and really start trusting in God. I have personally seen God make a way where there was no way. I have been blessed financially when I knew no one to help me.

The specialist claimed I was getting much worse, so they wanted me to see psychologists. I started seeing a psychologist, and I told him that in a short amount of time I was going to be healed. Well, he wanted to know where I got that kind of faith. I explained to him what I heard the Holy Spirit say, and I just knew that was the truth, so there was no point in being overly concerned about it. He tried to convince me that I was not in good shape at all, but since that had no effect on me, we became more like friends to the point that we discussed our hopes and dreams and what we wanted to accomplish in life.

Finally my wife and I found a new church to start going to in this new city and state. Things started out okay at this church, but something just kept bothering me every time I got around the pastor, so I made it a point after a couple of weeks to try to get to know him. I knew I had no Bible College and I didn't know the Scriptures all that well, l but I knew if I just listened for what the Spirit of God would have me say, I would be okay. I sat down with this pastor and was listening in my spirit to what the Spirit of God would have me say. So I said, "Pastor, what do you do on your days off from here?"

He cheerfully stood up and said, "I put on magic shows."

Immediately the Spirit of God rose up in me and I said, "White or black magic isn't any different, because the Word of God says magic is evil." At that, he straightened up in his seat and yelled at me! I could see pride coming forth out from him like a tidal wave. After that, I really wasn't welcomed back to his church.

Too many Christians are afraid to question their pastor. It's like people get this idea that their pastor is supreme and his word is the final authority. I don't believe that, nor do I believe in leaving a church just because of something that was said. If a pastor is a true man of God, the people should walk in humility toward him, but ask questions. One should not attack a pastor or otherwise his defenses will be up. If there is a problem, one should go to him with humility and he can explain. But one shouldn't allow a pastor to sugarcoat what the Scriptures call *sin*.

I read an article in a magazine that claimed that what God called magic in the book of Exodus and the magic of today are not the same, so we can't go by the same guidelines as are in the Bible. This teaching is completely from the pit of hell. I don't care how you sugarcoat it, trickery is trickery.

Well, I ended up in several more emergency rooms because my spasms were out of control. More specialists were confused about why my body wasn't getting either better or worse like they were expecting. I ended up becoming good friends with a doctor that said, "Okay, nothing is doing any good, and I have taken a special interest in you now because I see you having a bright future. But I don't know what I can do." So he started treating me with supplements and high doses of vitamins that were all natural. To his amazement and to mine, I soon started feeling much better. Pretty soon I was quite a bit healthier, and I didn't have to go to emergency rooms much at all anymore. I was feeling a lot better. Within six months I was no longer going to emergency rooms at all, and I was walking just fine. Within a year, it was exciting, because I could throw a football and I was running again. Within sixteen months, I was doing so well that we decided to live around our families again, so we moved back to our home town. Throughout the whole time, I kept in the Word, but the spirit of suicide didn't give up at all, and I still had to face many challenges.

While facing these challenges in life with the spirit of suicide constantly attacking me, I was learning that if I stayed humble, God's grace and mercy would like a river flow over me. Many demonic attacks kept coming, and I could see there was a purpose to all of this. Because of familiar spirits, I was being attacked day and night, and we weren't sure where to go, so we kept praying about it. My wife was getting hit hard to the point she didn't think she could handle it. Then one night I cried out for wisdom, because we were experiencing strange things. We were seeing shadows move around and items were getting lost mysteriously.

The Spirit of God took me deep into the spiritual realm, and I saw a baby running around our bed at night blaspheming Jesus Christ, so I took authority over it and pleaded the blood of Jesus over our bed and over our apartment, and within a short period of time, the attacks stopped.

We decided to go ahead and move to another state that we thought would be great to live in and started making the arrangements. I went to my pastor, but he didn't agree at all. In fact he was upset at me for wanting to move. Please understand that this pastor knew I had the prophetic gift on my life to where I could hear from God, so he often used my gift a lot to help himself out, but he didn't want to hear what God was saying for himself. Things were going good at this church and using my gift was exciting, but I didn't realize that there was going to be an all-out war taking place. A spiritual war broke out that no one was prepared for.

When this pastor needed a financial breakthrough or someone in the church needed money, they would ask me to pray to see what God would say. Many people, including my pastor, were greatly blessed by my telling them what I thought God said to do. Well, the enemy came in like a flood and my pastor blamed me for most of it. It turned out very sad, because a lot of things were put on me and I was blamed for a lot of the demonic attacks on the church. Almost everything I saw, looking back now after several years, was caused from lack of spiritual maturity and no one walking in humility. The Word of God is very clear about this: humility goes before honor, but pride goes before destruction. I also realize now that I may have been operating through the spirit of divination without realizing it.

I can't stress enough that if you want more of God and more of the things of God, you have to walk in humility. Look at Micah 6:8. God requires us to walk in humility. Even if that lesson took me down in despair, I praise God it happened, because I didn't realize just how evil pride is until I walked in it. I was walking away from God because of it, and I didn't even realize it. One thing

I have learned is that the greater the anointing you have, the greater amount of humility you must walk in.

The pastor and I reconciled after that and things got a lot better. Before we moved, another pastor I knew was really stepping out in faith to see what God was wanting him to do, so we started praying for him a lot. The Spirit of God said to us, "Help him out. Be his servant." So my wife and I began doing everything we could. I started to prophesy again and we were seeing great things happen.

But I knew it was time to leave that state, so I went to the pastor and he gave us his blessing and we moved. As we went down the highway, curses were being broken off my life, and I began experiencing a freedom I had never known before. I felt like the Spirit of God was rising up in me and saying, "I am well pleased with you now. Walk in your freedom."

I then made a horrible financial decision, thinking it was time that I go into the ministry. I thought that now I was ready. But God showed me that there was more pride that needed to be destroyed out of me, so we ended up with no destination, living in a motel for three days. I was severely humbled, but, praise God, with his mercy we ended up going back to Him. You see, many people claim to love God, but a major part of loving God that most people don't want to talk about is trusting God even when it makes no sense. Jesus said in Matthew 15:8: "They draw near to me and honor me with their lips but their heart is far from me."

I have seen more Christians submit to the spirit of fear than I have seen be victorious. See, we as Christians need to realize that when we do anything in life, we should walk by faith and not by sight. 2 Corinthians 5:7 When God is asking you to move here or there, or He's asking you to do this or that, and you don't, you must come to the point that you realize you're in pride. God has asked me to do several things in life at times, and I chose not to do them mainly because of fear. The spirit of fear is a bully and likes intimidating people, especially God's people. He has been doing this for thousands of years.

One time I experienced something that to this day really surprises me. My wife and I were in an unbearable circumstance where all hope was pretty much gone. We wanted just to explode at God, but decided rather to praise Him and continue to praise Him, even though all hope was gone. Well, it was like Jesus Christ himself came in to our living room. My wife started to pray with more boldness, and I started to worship God in tongues. We were in one of the worst of circumstances, but it turned around so fast that I could literally see every demon that was attacking us running away, because they knew the power of God had hit our place so hard that my wife and I were transformed. We had begun speaking more boldly of God instead of giving in to discouragement. I had to really come to a point in my life where I asked, "Will I serve a demon, or will I serve the living God?" No one can make that decision for you. In John 14:15, Jesus said, "If you love me, keep my commandments."

If you say you love Jesus, then you must learn to trust him. Many Satanist and occultist will tell you the most dangerous person is the person who really trusts God. When a person humbles himself to the level to where he trusts God, he has such an enormous amount of power on his side that the demons get scared of him. Most people don't realize it, but Satan doesn't care if they *believe* in God or not. Satan's only concern is if they *serve* the living God or not. John 10:10 says that Satan came to steal, kill and destroy. But Jesus came to give us life and life more abundantly. There are many so-called Christians that are actually living for Satan, because a true Christian will pick up his cross and walk in this new life daily. To understand this, just look to Christ and how he lived. The day we start living for ourselves is the day we start living for Satan.

Look at the greatest commandment, "Love the Lord your God with all your heart, strength, soul and mind." Satan hates all humans because God sent his Son to die for them. But Satan especially hates a true Christian, because a true believer lives for the living God who severely humbled him. A Christian that submits under the power of God is the most powerful weapon in the universe, and Satan knows this. So if you want to harm Satan's kingdom, submit your life fully to God. Maybe you have noticed that it seems that Satan doesn't seem to bother much with the majority of lukewarm Christians. Most lukewarm Christians I know get the great jobs, have plenty of worldly success, are rapidly promoted in the business world and even in the local church. The god of this world is doing a very good job at blinding many people from seeing the truth. I have personally met a number of pastors who believe that if a person is financially doing well, they must be in good with God. It's amazing how many Christians I know believe this also. Satan is not against the exalting of lukewarm Christians, because they have very little direct effect on his kingdom.

When I was trying to get help and get out of occult practices, many so-called Christians didn't want me in their life. I was told I would bring demonic attacks on their church, so I had to leave. One time my wife and I were attending a church, and major attacks were coming on our lives. We didn't know what to do, so we went to our pastors, and they said that they had handed us over to Satan to be destroyed because of my past. Not only did they not have any right to do this, but the price they will pay for being leaders and saying such a thing is going to be far intense at judgment day than for the lukewarm Christians in their congregations. We, as Christians, need to decide just whom we will serve and honor.

Proverbs 1:7 says that the fear of the Lord is the beginning of wisdom. Even though we ended back where we started, God had all things planned out for us to be blessed. For several years I was terrified of computers and was told to apply to a certain company, because they needed sales people, so I applied and was quickly hired. Well, no one told me I had to work with computers, so when I started training I just wanted to quit, but the Spirit of God seemed to say in my heart, "You need this training for where I am going to take you later on." So I admitted to the Lord that I didn't know a thing.

Well, a lot of people there looked down on me and several ridiculed me, but the company told me that if I was willing to learn for free, they would spend time every day after class teaching me what I would need to know. Since then I have talked at churches and given my testimony and not only told people to walk in humility, but have lived it in many ways. The more I have humbled myself before God, the more God has exalted me. I ended up learning a lot about computers, and through that experience, I have seen God bless me beyond my wildest dreams. I won several sales contests and was blessed in so many ways because God's favor was on me.

After about three years and learning about computers and helping a pastor out plus leading people to Christ and making sure they were on solid ground with the Lord should an attack from the enemy come, we sensed that God was going to send us elsewhere. One day as I was sitting behind my computer, the Spirit of God came on me and said, "I am moving you back East." When I told my wife about this, she was not excited at all. But she knew in her heart that God wanted to train us for the ministry, and there really wasn't anyone there to help us. You see, where I am from, most pastors never send anyone out to get trained for the ministry or even encourage it. It's strange, but they get this idea that they know how to run other people's lives and whatever they think is the direct will of God.

After we committed to go to wherever God wanted us to go, I had another major car accident. I knew then that things had to change, so we started praying to learn what things we needed answers for. The more we submitted to God, the more Satan attacked, but we didn't know who to contact for help so we decided to write to different ministries and get a lot of prayer going on our behalf. Then God started to really show me that I was called to do great things for His kingdom, but Satan was trying to destroy me in every way, so I needed to spend more time in prayer and really seek out the will of God in each area of my life.

Then one day as I was drinking my morning coffee, the Spirit of God took me up into the third heaven and showed me what the blood of Christ has done for all mankind. The Spirit of God said, "You need to understand the power of the blood, and what Jesus Christ's name means. Colossians 2:15 points out that Jesus disarmed the principalities and powers and made a public spectacle of them, triumphing over them."

So I started pleading the blood of Jesus Christ over my finances, my car, my life and everything in it. Then the Spirit of God said, "Satan has open access to attack you through demonic soul ties that are not of God. Those doors need to be closed." I realized then that many people from my past had not been healthy for me, so the Spirit of God showed me I needed to repent of specific things in my past. I repented of all the women I had had immoral relations with and all the occult activity I had been was in. Then I asked God to sever the ties from several relationships that I had had in high school.

I had committed idolatry with a woman I wanted to marry, to where this woman actually became a god to me. After repenting initially when we first come to Christ, we still have to work on our past. We need to go back and repent for specific things we said or did many years ago. (Luke 6:47-49) I felt so many weights fall off of me. For the first time since my brother's death, I felt like chains were being taken off me. For the first time, I felt condemnation and hopelessness leave me. Also, I felt the deepening of my loving relationship with God. When I shouted "Freedom in Jesus Christ," I actually heard what sounded like demonic spirits squealing like pigs in pain and scrambling off.

After all the mess of the car accident was taken care of, we finally picked a date to leave. Please note that of all the car accidents I have been in, only one was my fault. Many Christians, even our pastor, said about this, "I don't believe this is of God. You need to stay here." Others said, "Well, when I see you in a year, you will know I was right. It wasn't of God." I think that too many people in leadership or in a position in the church are not very sensitive to the Spirit of God.

Many times people tried to put the fear of man or the fear of failure on me, but I refused to allow that to turn me away from God's leading in my life. Often people project their own fears onto their children, or their close friends. Don't try to stop the power of God from flowing, because you don't want to get in God's way. I have seen so many people afraid to leave their hometown, or afraid to leave the church they grew up in, that I really wonder what God they serve. A friend of mine was afraid of success. His son got on the honor roll, and it bothered him. Why would any parent hold back their child from wanting to succeed?

Well, we needed some help with finances in order to be able to leave, but I knew to trust God. So as an act of faith, I started packing, and my wife was surprised that I was packing to leave, and she knew we needed help financially. My father called me and asked how things were going, and the Spirit of God said, "Be honest with him all the way." So I said, "Dad, we don't have the same beliefs, but I believe great things will happen to us back North, and we need some help with the money." My father is not the type of person that just hands out money, especially a lot of money. I have not ever seen him do this. But when he asked, "How much do you need?", I told him and he gave a lot more than we were expecting.

Our move was a lot easier than many expected, because before I had the money, the Spirit of God said, "Go ahead and pack everything you don't use on a daily basis." So our place looked like a stuffed garage for over a month, but I knew God was going to come through. The Word of God is very clear about this. Faith without action is dead. Let me explain something here so you, the reader, can better understand. Two men needed a job and both were praying about getting a job. One sent out his resumé and spent the money to do this; the other man said, "I have faith, but I am not spending any money," so he didn't send out his resumé. Which one had the faith to get a job?

As we were on the highway the Holy Spirit said, "I am leading you to a place of more than abundance, but first you must go into the desert to learn more". Many Christians don't understand this, but where did the Holy Spirit take Christ? Into the desert, because that is where you can grow and learn a lot about trusting God. Well, my wife and I went through two years of very difficult times. The first six months, my wife almost wanted to give up, because we had several self-righteous Christians look down on us. And then we had many secular people mock us as well. But I knew that something was about to break wide open, and we were going to be blessed.

We had lived in a place that was spiritually dead, and nobody ever said, "Wow! So and so came from that kind of a life and got saved!" It was a place where people wanted only what was best for them and sin ran rampant in the churches. God has blessed us so much since we humbled ourselves and left that area. We have been living in the same state and city now for six years as of this writing, and we have seen God bless us more than I would ever think. If anyone thinks part of my life has been easy, they are sadly mistaken. Most of my life has been one demonic attack after another one, and it seems like I have been in countless battles to the point I have gone without food, and tears became a big part of my life with no sign of relief, of any hope in sight. But when people ask me what I would have changed, I tell them that I would have changed nothing, because the pain and suffering I endured has made me love God that much more.

Luke 7:47 says that those who have been forgiven much love much. That is why I wouldn't change a thing, because I have a deep love for Jesus Christ. He is as real a person as I am. There were times I was so stressed out that I could not eat or sleep, and I was in complete misery, but it was through those times that I could feel God's love showering me with His presence. The more one time spends with God, the more one will love Him and see just how real He is.

My life is by no means perfect, but God is perfect in every way. We cannot comprehend Him, but just to taste a part of God's love will transform one into being more like Him. Many Christians ask me why I expose my dark secrets to people that I don't know. The answer is simple. The more I die to self, the greater Jesus Christ can and will be exalted through me. I realize that this book is going to cause some people to reject me. But that is okay, because I only seek to let Christ be glorified through this book.

The Word of God states that if Christ lives in me, and I live in him, and he died on the cross for me, then my life doesn't really belong to me, because I was bought with his precious blood on a horrible cross that He didn't deserve. I know it wasn't God's will for me to fall into so much evil, nor was it God's will for so many churches to reject me, but through all the heartache I have been through, Jesus Christ is exalted, for I can see just how far He reached out His hand to help me.

Jesus will do the same for you if you just say, "Jesus, I need you", and you're willing to humble yourself and say, "I am done. It's time I give my life over to you." For the first time in my life, I have friends that call me now just to say "hi" or see how I am doing. And now I have people that call me and ask me for prayer or advice. Most of my life with Jesus Christ, when I exposed my past to people, it caused almost everyone to treat me like I was a pariah. Some even tried to be the Holy Spirit by trying to do His job, but that isn't of God. I, like most people, just want to be treated with respect and as an equal, not an inferior.

Out of the six states I have lived in and the twenty churches I have been to, probably I know at least fifteen pastors really well and at least one hundred fifteen Christians really well. I can say that only about seven people treated me really well. Now, for the first time after nearly twenty years of seeking the Lord, I have a mentor who is a real spiritual father to me. I find this man so incredible because his past life was nothing like mine, yet he has shown my family and me so much kindness that we are amazed.

For a long time I believed that when someone was really spiritually mature, they couldn't be close to someone like me, but I discovered that this was a lie, because look at Christ's life. He was very close to very ungodly people. Also this man has become a very dear friend and my mentor who calls me just to see how things are going in my life. I have a pastor to that hears from the Holy Spirit. At times I may not like his opinion, but I still greatly respect him. One thing I respect dearly about my mentor and my pastor is that they encourage people to really go after the things of God.

Some pastors appear to be sitting on their thrones treating people like they are children, but not these men of God. They encourage people to do what God says to do. It took years of seeking after God before we ended up at a place where we are truly loved and accepted. But there will always be Christian people who are spiritually immature and who will reject people because of their past. This is going to happen, because the religious spirit is everywhere. Remember it was the religious spirit that lied to the religious leaders of the Jews during the time of Jesus. The Pharisees and religious leaders were the ones who instigated to have Christ killed. Later on I will discuss the religious spirit in greater detail.

For many years I didn't have close bonds with anyone, because the minute people found out about my past or I would share part of my life with people, the stones would start flying. It's sad to say, but most Christians are afraid of psychics, witches, warlocks, Satanists, or occultists. If one doesn't understand the power or authority one has in Christ, one should by no means be in any responsible position of leadership. The power of Christ's blood is much greater by far than anyone can fathom, and like the Word says, Jesus Christ's name is above every name. Many pastors I know don't want to engage in spiritual warfare, because it comes at a cost. Some don't even want to mention the word "sin". They are like the New Age movement that says, "If it feels good and looks good, it must be okay, because it's from God."

These pastors don't ask you to repent and grow. No one will question you about if you are growing spiritually. A pastor I once knew asked God to please use him. Well, God gave this man the opportunity to launch huge outreach to young people, but because these kids dyed their hair orange, blue and green, he wasn't interested in that kind of outreach. All Christians should want to be used by God, but they can't tell the Creator how to use them. If you can't handle kids that dye their hair, what's going to happen when a person goes into a church and starts barking? I have actually seen someone foam at the mouth and bark right in a service.

Years ago when somebody didn't want to believe me about my past, I called up a demon, and he saw a shadow. It scared him badly, but then I realized how I can't serve God and still communicate with demons. I hate to say this, but a majority of the pastors I know are very weak in the faith. I didn't understand why some people called themselves pastors when they seemed so weak, but I realized that if they will humble themselves, God is willing to help them to fulfill their calling.

When Jesus was on earth, many begged him to heal this or that person, so he went all over. Pastors nowadays have it easy. The demon-possessed come to them for counseling, or those oppressed by the enemy are in their congregation, but the pastor nowadays is often too afraid to even lift a finger to help such a person. I have been personally rejected so many times because people were bound by fear in the church. I just wanted to be accepted and loved and just have someone to listen to me, but time after time I was asked to leave the church or I was treated like an inferior being.

That's one of the reasons I decided to write this book, because I serve a God that loves, restores and heals. God's Word says, "If my people will humble themselves and seek my face, I will heal their land and restore them." Many people talk about revival, but I believe we will not see a revival in America until God's people start walking in love and humbling themselves and repenting of their sins and the sins we have allowed to go on in the church. We, as Christians, must take a stand against the principalities and powers of darkness that reign over this lost world. Second Timothy says that the lord will deliver us from every evil work and preserve us for his heavenly kingdom. Wow! Wouldn't it be great to know a pastor that wasn't bound by fear, but live the Word?

Satan will always attack. We know this, but we serve someone greater than Satan, and that is why we can shout with victory, because we have the precious blood of Jesus Christ, and we have Jesus Christ's name to help us. Many Christians can quote the first part of John 10:10, but let's focus our attention on the next part: Jesus came to give us life and life more abundantly. Too many Christians worry and get all stressed out when Satan attacks. Jesus has the answer if one will just be still and listen.

Years ago I had the transmissions break down in two different cars, and my finances were being hit hard. Then a man I thought was a friend came to me and said, "The battle over you is too intense, and I can't have you in my life any longer." My wife and I were in great shock because we were left without a way to get to church, but we knew to stand strong, though we were being hit from every direction. So I decided to do the best thing. I went to my Father in heaven. I learned long ago not to go directly to the pastor, because most pastors speak what they see in the natural. So I don't go to a pastor first. I go directly to my heavenly Father.

God loves you, my friend, and He cares about you. God created you, and he knows all things and sees all things. Too many Christians call Jesus "Lord", but look what Jesus said in Luke 6:46: "Why do you call me Lord and not do the things which I say?" God is speaking. Do you hear him? Pray and seek God out, and you will be so grateful you did. When you are in a situation, and you don't know what to do, seek God out diligently with prayer and in his Word. If Jesus Christ were to stand before you and say, "Would you go here or there or would you give up this job and take that job?" would you do it? If Jesus asked you to do something, could you do it without complaining and whining? Philippians 2:14 Once God's loving Holy Spirit asked me to go to work at a certain construction company. At first I thought that was not going to work out, because I had been a salesman, but I took the job not knowing why. When God opens the door wide open, it's of God. So I didn't know why I was there.

I had to walk in a lot of humility, because I didn't know why I was there, and most everyone there was twice my size. Well, I had a major problem with my walkie-talkie, so I had to be trained on it, but I gained favor from a man that most people were afraid of, because he was the lead foreman. He often would mock people for their dumb mistakes. He and I actually became friends, and one day he opened up to me. Right then and there I knew why God had asked me to take that job. That man was full of hurt and needed someone to just pour love into him--Christ's love, that is. Well, in a month I was promoted and given a great position. As I built up a friendship with this man, I was able to share part of my life with him. Then he shared a horribly sad story to me about his life, so I talked to him about God's forgiveness. He shed a tear with me, and at that moment the ice around this man's heart broke. Well, I knew it was time for me to leave that company, but every now and then, I call him to see how he's doing. He always so excited to talk to me.

You see, I don't want to just talk about God's love, I want to show it! This man loved heavy equipment, and it's what was most important in his life, so I allowed this man to teach me a lot. The funny thing about him is that I heard he could eat nails and feel no pain. God is looking for someone to get out of themselves and walk in obedience to what He's asking them to do. If you're not sure what to do, seek out wise counsel! That may not be from a pastor. Wise counsel is often found in a group of people, and this may or may not include your pastor. But don't just take their advice. In the book of Joshua we can learn a lot. Look at Joshua 9:1-27 but the place I want you to see is verse 14. We need to have wise counsel at all times, even when things are going great in our lives. Also, remember to go to Christ daily, because he is mindful of you. Psalms 115:12 God loves you and is watching over you daily and thinking about you.

If you think you don't know how to pray, just start talking to God about the things that are important to you in life. God is listening, and He is waiting for you just to speak to Him. God wants you to seek after Him, not after the things of this world, not riches. That is why when we pray, we say, "God, may your will be done, not my will."

Too many Christians run after this or that and then end up really confused to where they make a lot of wrong decisions. God is not a God of confusion. But when you seek to please yourself, you will end up confused, because God must be first in your life. When I began to walk with God, the Holy Spirit spoke to me saying, "My child, why are you so afraid?" I can only respond, "God, may Your will be done."

Because of all the evil I have done, I once thought God would strike me dead if I should say, "God, Your will be done." It took me almost a year to say that. When we became homeless and lived in a motel for three days with nowhere to go, I was mad at God, but God showed me that I had put up boundaries marking just how far I would trust Him. God wanted to crush all my fears and show me that He is a God that loves me, and He doesn't lie. So I had to repent of my pride, because when we don't trust God, we are in pride. One thing I needed to learn was that godly sorrow produces repentance which leads to salvation. 2 Corinthians 7:10 If God didn't discipline me, my pride would have sent me to hell. So I praise God that He loves me enough to humble me to where I didn't position myself to be destroyed.

If you want your dreams and hopes fulfilled, then seek out God, and He will help you. But let me warn you of this: if you want to see the blessings stop coming in your life and your life filled with problems, fall into pride. It was pride that caused Satan to fall from the will of God. If there is one sin that has brought down more ministries and churches than any other, it is pride. We as Christians must avoid pride at all cost. Look at Second Timothy 3:1-5. Our society promotes pride, and more people are falling into it now than at any other time. But look closely at verse five: "Having a form of godliness but denying its power." He is talking to the Church. This should put the fear of God in us all.

CHAPTER 3

A New Hope

After arriving in a new place, my wife and I didn't know where God was leading us to go to church or where to work. But God had everything planned out, and it was incredible. My oldest daughter suggested that we call a prayer line for prayer. My wife called and the woman who answered was so great to talk to. She said, "We have a service tonight at my church!" So my wife got the directions, and we went to church the first night we were in this new city.

We were excited about going to church, and the ministry there really encouraged us. We hadn't heard that kind of preaching before. At the end of the service, they asked if anyone needed prayer, so my wife and oldest daughter went forward. The prayer partner asked my daughter if we were new to the church. To our amazement, the woman that had given my wife directions over the phone turned out to be the same person standing before my wife and daughter! That was surprise enough, but what took place next was so bizarre that only God could do it.

The prayer partner was so excited that she asked me to come down front too, and then called for the senior pastor to come meet us. It turned out that he had been awakened very early in the morning by our prayer partner saying that a family from out of town was relocating to the city and needed him to help them get established. The church we were in had about ten thousand members. It was not a small church at all!

Where I am from, a big church has about a thousand members. The service I was in that evening had about three thousand people in attendance, so it really surprised me that this pastor would really want to meet me. I was again amazed that this pastor should treat me with so much love, genuine concern, and great respect. We sat down and talked for about an hour, and I was careful to tell him exactly the way it was with no exaggeration in any way. I sensed that he had the anointing of God resting on him. He talked in such a loving way, but with such great authority.

This pastor helped us in so many ways! I couldn't begin to tell you how much he reached out to us. We were assigned a care pastor who was also patient, loving and kind. I felt like crying, because that's what I had been looking for all my life. I told the senior pastor about my past to test him to see if he could still love and accept me, and to my surprise, he gave me a hug which I will never forget. There I was, a wretched man with really no hope, because Satanic attacks kept coming against me. I was suffering horrible nightmares, plus I had been beaten down by other pastors, so I had a lot of baggage. After we talked, he prayed over me, and right then and there, I felt the power of God course through me in a mighty way to where I felt the demons around me shutter with fear.

We moved into a nice place soon, and I got a job right away. One very important thing I need to point out here is that when God's loving Holy Spirit asks you to do something, the Word of God will back it up. I have met many people who claimed God said to do this or that, but it was against his Word. God loves his Word and protects his Word so much that he will not ever go against it, because he guards it and loves it that much. Matthew 5:18-18; 24:35 Many people have told me they were told not to work, but just do the work of the ministry. But when I would point out that Paul made tents on the mission field, they just got very upset. If your bills are stacking up, and you're bringing a lot of hardship on your family, you really need to seek out wise counsel. You see, when God asks me to do something, He always provides the way, not always what I like necessarily, but He still provides it. When we do what God asks us to do, He doesn't just meet us half-way, He goes all the way to meet every need we have.

A couple that my wife and I knew told us that the Holy Spirit said for them to move to California, but they refused. So again the Holy Spirit had someone tell they that they were to move to California. Then they said, "We can't believe we have lost our jobs and things have been really difficult for us here." But I pointed out to them that since Christ died for us, we should live for him and not for ourselves.

Being in rebellion to God is the same as being in witchcraft. Many Christians don't seem to like to acknowledge the whole Word of God. Like I stated before, Satan's number one task is to get a Christian to be in disobedience to God. We need to come to a place that we start humbling ourselves and saying, "Not my will, but Your will be done."

As we see in scripture, Jesus Christ didn't want to go to the cross, but he did, because he gave us the example to live by "not my will but Your will be done." All Satan wants is for people to come against God's will, because Satan knows that God has a perfect plan for us to be blessed in every area of our lives, and if we are in God's will, we are being set up for great success, and God's holy protection will be upon us.

When God told Abraham to move, He didn't tell him all that was going to happen. He just told him to leave the area he was from. Many times God will ask us to leave the area we are from because familiar spirits there constantly remind us of past sins. They have no mercy, and there is no grace in them at all. Even though you try to block them out of your mind, they are very evil and will constantly attack.

Familiar spirits really like it when you get bored or lonely, because that is when they launch their full-scale attack. I have met people that moved back to their home area and within a short time, their walk with God was destroyed. Familiar spirits make you believe you're condemned and not worth anything at all. I have known people who were full of the joy of the Lord and moved back home. Within days they were depressed, but didn't know why.

We, as Christians, must realize that we're in a battle, and Satan is going to use whatever he can to pull you away from the will of

God. I have personally had to deal with familiar spirits countless times that tried to convince me to move back home. They like to work on your emotions, because they are in the soulish realm. But it's like a friend of mine. He submitted to these spirits, moved back home, and within a week I learned about how much of a failure he was, and how he had turned against God. He actually got involved in bestiality. Wicked, evil spirits have power, and if we give them a foothold in our lives, they can give us a powerful illusion.

Just think how many people have gone so far as to kill their own children thinking they were doing God's will. Too many people think that playing with spirits is just a game or that going to see a psychic is just for fun, but people don't realize that when that one spiritual door is opened like that, the enemy can take control of their mind.

I slit my wrist, and didn't even know what was really happening until I realized my shirt had blood all over it. You see, Charles Manson, Ted Bundy, Adolf Hitler, and the list goes on and on, all opened themselves up to demonic powers. At first it is a lot of fun and seems harmless, but you don't realize how evil it is until one day you wake up, and you can no longer think normally.

Many years ago before I got saved, I used to meditate on killing a certain person. I believe if it had not been for God's grace having me get locked up, I would have killed that person and not even realized it. See, when I would have out-of-body experiences, I would think, "Wow! This is so great! I am able to move objects with my spirit-man." But what was happening was that since I wasn't protected by Christ's blood, those spirits I was harboring could convince me of anything. I was literally going insane, and there's no doubt about it, because as time went on I got really confused between what was tangible reality and what was not. I must say that I did enjoy it a lot, but there were times when people looked at me and said, "Who are you?"

A friend of mine from high school spent a lot of time with me, and for some reason I became physically attracted to him. God warns us that if we don't stop our sin he will hand us over to a depraved mind. Well, my friend found out about it and that was the last time I talked to him and that was years ago. So we need to be aware that demonic parlor games are not to be taken lightly. People have asked me if it is okay to read the horoscope. My response has been that many things seem to start off harmless, but then you find yourself going one step further and then another step still further. See, demons like to entice us, so the first time might be okay, but the second or third time is all it takes for Satan to get a foothold. All it takes is for Satan to have the legal ground to just a foothold. And we give it to him when we play his games!

Whenever we claim God said this or that, we had better make sure that we have the fear of God in us. I have met people that said God told them to divorce their spouse and marry some other person. We need to understand that God loves His Word and He protects it. I have seen people come under a curse and the door was wide open for Satan to attack, and they got others to believe the same lie they did. In the Word it says that even if an angel comes and gives you another gospel, you are not to believe it. Galatians 1:8-9, Isaiah 8:20

The Bible severely limits justifiable reasons to divorce. But we live in a society that loves to promote humanism. That is a real fancy word for New Age. When we tell the Creator what part of His Holy Word we will follow and what laws we will obey, we are far from being Christ-like. Jesus said it very clearly: "If you love me, obey my commandments." If you have no real interest in serving Jesus Christ, then this whole book may be meaningless to you. Serving Jesus Christ may seem to be the hardest thing you can do, but the blessings of knowing and serving the living God are far beyond anything Satan has to offer.

Well, we attended this mega-church for about eighteen months, but I knew I needed more help that I was getting there, because I kept having demonic dreams and visitations. My wife had a good friend that gave her a booklet about soul ties. I studied the book and ended up being led to repenting of many more of the specific sins that I had committed. I had never heard of ungodly soul ties until I really dived into the Word of God. It's amazing how having sex outside of marriage can open a door to strong demonic attacks. I started asking God to sever all past relationships with all those with whom I had had demonic emotional strongholds

As a result, I started getting free, and it was amazing how I could see changes taking place in me, and how I was becoming a lot happier as a person. For a long time, I would fall into a demonic trance to where my I did things that could have gotten me killed. One time I remember driving down the highway with my eyes wide open, but the spirit of suicide tried to convince me to drive off the highway and just end it all. My car would start to swerve in a way where I would end up dying. So through that book about soul ties, I got set free of the demonic trances that I would fall into.

The pastor of the mega church asked me to keep contact with him, and I still do to this very day. I believe he did everything for me he knew to do, but because I had dabbled so much in such deep wickedness, I don't think he knew how to really help me. Well, we started attending another church that taught a lot about spiritual warfare, and we enjoyed it a lot, plus we were growing in Christ. We began to be blessed in mighty ways, and I was being liberated from a lot more confusion, and things were going great.

Then one day we noticed that the senior pastor wasn't talking to his members. We weren't used to this, because I have always liked meeting with my pastor. We stayed even though we thought this was odd. But in time we remembered how Christ would talk to prostitutes and tax collectors, so why couldn't our pastor at least say "hi" to his own people. In time we realized nobody really was fellowshipping with other people. When we realized that people were no longer talking to each other before or after the service, we knew something was wrong. But what?

So we started seeking God about it, and the Holy Spirit directed us to something in the Bible that I must have read a hundred times, but never understood. It is found in 1 Corinthians 13:1: "Though I speak with the tongues of men and of angels, but have not love, I have become as a sounding brass or a clanging cymbal."

Why wouldn't a shepherd want to know his flock? We need to be Christ-like. Christ never had an attitude which sent the message that "I am better or more spiritual than you." My first pastor, Pastor Ted, and he always gives people time. He still sends me e-mails to this very day.

Well, the Holy Spirit said, "You don't belong in this church, so leave." But because I was being fed from the sermons, I figured I would just stay a little bit longer. Disobedience to God is never good, and it can cost you a lot. Shortly after that, I got into a really bad car accident. We prayed and decided we needed to let our pastor know about it. I was in shock when he refused to take any of my phone calls. We ran into some financial problems, but he still refused to take any of my calls. So we went to another church that could help us. They just loved on us a lot.

My new pastor asked us who our previous pastor had been. When we told him, he said it didn't surprise him that he acted that way, because the pastor where I had been for almost a year had the reputation of being too spiritual to get to know people unless they were in the full-time ministry. Our new pastor that helped us gave us the phone numbers of other pastors who could help us as well.

I finally decided to write our previous pastor a letter and express my hurt. I let him know how much we loved the church and wanted to come back. To my great surprise, he sent me a letter stating that I had a Jezebel spirit, and it was wrong for me to go to other churches for help. I wanted to write him again, but several pastors that I know personally counseled me to the effect that my original pastor was bound by pride, and you can't get through to a pastor like that. Only God can!

I will never forget how many ministries reached out to my wife and me with so much love, but every one of them asked me first, "Did you contact your pastor with this?" I told them that I had, but that he would never call back. After six months of this, I did eventually write to that pastor and apologize to him for telling other pastors that he didn't call me back, and I asked him again in that letter to let me know what he wanted me to do. But I didn't hear from him again.

We need to understand that some pastors don't understand what the call of God or anointing on their lives is. I know I could not ever be a pastor, because my pastor has a lot of patience and wisdom. Over time, he sees a lot of people come and go. I believe we need to pray a lot for our pastors, even when it seems that they aren't connecting with us. We should still pray a lot for them.

Sometimes I think my pastor doesn't care too much about me, but I can't let past thoughts or hurts control my life. Many times in my life the majority of God-haters were people who have been hurt by a pastor like him that refused to help them. It breaks my heart knowing there are God-haters around because a pastor hurt them.

But we must remember that pastors are human too, so we should never put our complete trust in them, but in God.

My pastor is on the front lines, and one thing I have discovered is that pastors don't get the credit they deserve, either. I have seen too many people attack their pastor or a pastor they had in the past. But what I tell people is that we must walk in forgiveness and realize there may be a lot of weak-minded pastors around, but there are also some genuine pastors like mine, who aren't always good at showing it, but they really do care.

The hardest part about this car accident I was in was that Satan tried to convince me that God's people don't care and that they are liars. Several times during this painful situation, a demon would come and stand before me and say, "If you will bow down and worship me, I will give you all that that you desire." See, Satan won't attack you when you're strong. He waits for when you let your guard down, and then he comes in like a roaring lion ready to devour you. 1 Peter 5:8 I have learned that when we are down spiritually, we must stand our ground and stand in faith. When things seem hopeless, you need to p.u.s.h......Pray.Until.Something.Happens! This might sound crazy, but I have had to do that many times in life. Just don't quit praying till the blessing manifests itself in the natural. I have had multiple excuses to give up on God, but like Peter said, "Lord, we have given up everything for you. Where else can we go?" John 6:67-68 If we are going to survive and carry our cross daily, we need to have Peter's attitude daily. So I pressed on, because I knew God wanted me to be free from all demonic curses from past sins and generational curses. God may not give you a perfect life, but He will give you a very fulfilling life if you just allow Him to.

Well, as God was faithfully healing my body, we bought three different cars, and each one broke down within six months after we bought them. I had many demons come and stand before me and say, "Just curse God, and give up on Him! He doesn't care!" Then a demon that looked like an angel of light came to me and said, "God sees your past, and you were predestined to serve Satan. But you're in rebellion, and that's why all this keeps happening to you."

My wife and I decided to praise God daily, because the attacks were getting worse and now our finances were down to the point where we just couldn't buy another car. In fact, we ended up going without a car for almost two years. Only once during that time did we have to carry the groceries home in the rain. And no matter what Satan threw at us, we stood against each demonic attack with tears running down our faces and without blaming God. There were times I was saying, "God, why are you allowing all this to happen to us?" But not once did we think God had abandoned us, because we knew God was going to bring restoration. Also, even though we may have had no car, we were getting favor from God in many other ways.

We found money. People would just want to bless us with money for no reason at all. One day a co-worker stopped by on our day off. My front door was open, so he walked in and threw a hundred dollar bill on the counter, then left. I was on the phone, so I asked him to hold on a minute, but he just got in his car and left. What surprised me more than anything about that was that he soon quit the company without saying good-bye to anyone. So it ended up that I didn't even get the chance to thank him for it! By all appearances, people could think we were in a horrible and hopeless situation, but God just kept bringing blessing into our home.

Many people said we needed help badly and were in desperate need. My thought is that if you want to see the hand of God move in your life, you need to be willing to humble yourself. One quick way to really get God's attention is to go out and help someone else. I have found myself doing things for others that normally I wouldn't do. And even if they didn't notice or say "thanks," God noticed what I did and that's what counts.

Well, we finally found another church. We were directed by the Holy Spirit to pray and intercede for those people, so we did. It was weird, because they wanted to know a lot about us, and we shared a little bit. Then one day it seemed like all the gates of hell were opened against our lives, and my wife and I fell into strife. I have told countless people, "If you ever want the blessings of God to stop in your house, fall into strife." Strife is the biggest blessing-killer there is, and the effects of this sin can be devastating for long periods of time. I have seen the spirit of strife destroy more marriages than any other spirit. This spirit is what causes people to lose their sanity, even kill their children out of rage and kill each another. James 3:16; 4:1-3

All peace and joy left my house. Then the Spirit of God came on me and said, "Be strong and of good courage in this very hour." Joshua 1:9. See, even though this was happening, God was making the point that we must trust Him and not lean on our own understanding. But remember, we need to walk in love, forgiveness and humility. It seemed like hell, but demonic strongholds were being broken off from us, and this made the enemy extremely mad. We continued to pray, but in so many ways I was ready to give up on God.

Then the next day, the Spirit of God started dealing with me like never before with great power, and said, "I gave you a heart to know me." Jeremiah 24:7 During this very painful season, we went to our pastors, and they suggested that we divorce. One of the biggest reasons I am writing this book is because there have been a lot of people like my wife and I who have been hurt by the church and want to blame God. I can feel your pain. But please realize that God loves you, and I am so deeply sorry that you have been hurt by those that should have loved you and protected you, but instead hurt you. I can't take away your pain. If I could, I would. But I can't. But I know a loving Friend and Savior than can. Jesus knows your pain, and he can feel it. Those that should have loved him and worshipped him spit on him, mocked him and crucified him.

Well, I wrote to a certain ministry and let them know what was happening, and they said that sometimes divorce is okay. I was in a world of pain and hurt because of all that was happening. I was going through a lot of confusion and turmoil. But God spoke to me and said, "Read my Word". He directed me to Isaiah 59:19: " When the enemy comes in like a flood, the spirit of the lord will lift up a standard against him." To my surprise, most of the things that were going on were caused by the beast himself. So we decided to press in to God much harder now. We spent many hours praying in the spirit and got the breakthrough we so desperately needed.

Then God's loving Holy Spirit showed my wife and me that Satan wanted to destroy our marriage because of the plans God had for us. It was amazing-- just like Job. God allowed Satan to come in like a flood to test us to see if we would abandon Him or if we would seek Him even more. Many Christians I have met have gone through very painful things and abandoned ship. But if there's one thing that God wants to make very clear in a Christian's life, it is that is Word is final! Christ said that many are called, but only a few are chosen. That's because there are only a few who will say, "God, your will be done." I have listened to hundreds of stories of why people gave up their calling or gave up on God, but none of their excuses are acceptable when we look at Christ did.

Too many pastors are afraid to talk about the blood of Jesus, sin, or the cross, because God's Word offends people. When a person who is gay, living in sin unmarried, or supports abortion, can attend a church without repenting, I don't even have to ask what's being preached there, because the cross will offend people no matter what their sin may be. It breaks my heart when a Christian claims abortion is no sin, because there are so many scripture that point out that all children are special to God, have a purpose from God for their life, and that God knows us before we are even born. When a pastor or a leader of a ministry start speaking words that are contrary to the Bible, we must stand strong and humble ourselves. Trusting in God is by no means easy, but it's so worth it if you will just press on. Jesus said, "I will never leave you nor forsake you," so please take this to heart. I don't know what you, the reader, may be going through right now, but I can say this: Jesus Christ has the answer, no matter how big the problem seems.

Many people claim to be Christian, but true disciples of Christ are humble, have the fear of God in their heart, and are concerned about what they say and do to others. I have met some very cold and ruthless people in the church who claimed to be Christians but were nothing like Christ. Even in my own church, there are people who are very self-righteous. One can tell that by just looking at the way they talk and act around others. This is a problem in every church.

There will always be people who believe they are really something. What most Christians don't realize is that this is a religious spirit. Religious spirits in the scriptures were mainly on the Pharisees and Sadducees. I actually enjoy talking to most God-haters if they will be honest with me, because their story of being hurt by some so-called Christian is in almost every conversation. Because so many phony people have come into my life, I ask God to reveal their heart to me.

Christ humbled Himself and left paradise to come to earth knowing that he was going to suffer and die. John 6:51 Yet many so-called Christians are judging their friends on what type a car they drive or what kind of a home they live in. This is real. This is really happening in the church. When we have been rejected, betrayed, hurt or lied to, sometimes the last thing we think about is praying. But if you will humble yourself, God will pour out his compassion, sensitivity, mercy, grace and love on you. Within a short time you will feel restored. The worst thing you can do is let this pain turn into bitterness.

I have met people who were very bitter, and it was so sad, because almost every one of them was severely lonely and without much hope in life. What I find so amazing about bitterness is how it's like drinking poison while hoping the other person will die. There have been countless times I have been rejected and deeply hurt by Christians. But as humbling as it is, how can I really stand in judgment of them when Christ was being beaten and crucified while he was saying, "Lord, forgive them, for they know not what they do." Luke 14:15 See, Jesus was asking God the Father to forgive those who were beating him to death and crucifying him.

I can't tell you how many times I have had a pastor look down on me because of my past, or how many times Christians looked down on my wife and me because we lived in a rented apartment or drove around in an older car. See, we, as Christians, need to realize that if we will give up worldly things and seek godliness, we will receive persecution. 2 Timothy 3:12 I didn't have to seek God out to get things, because I could have gone to college, but the Spirit of God had other plans for me. Many Christians have their own agendas, but like I said before, Jesus said, "If you love me, keep my commandments." John 14:15

Sometimes God is asking you to go on the mission field, or become a pastor. But if you don't give God all your heart, you're not going to know His will. Many have asked me where all my boldness and joy come from. That's easy! The Word says that the joy of the lord is my strength. Jesus Christ is just as real to me as my wife is. I desire so much for people to know him. When I have gotten down before God, humbled myself and looked to the Word, the Holy Spirit has led me to Joel 3:10: "Let the weak say I am strong." Many times with no hope in sight, I have had to stand in faith alone. Most pastors I have met seem very weak in their faith, especially if it's an attack by demonic spirits. This is not to condemn them. It's just like I pointed out before. I believe that too many people are in leadership that shouldn't be where they are. Sometimes to do battle, we need great faith.

In the Bible it says that God is the author and finisher of our faith. Because God is love we as Christians need to understand that God wants the very best for us. He sent His only-begotten Son to die for us. But we must fight the good fight of faith, because Satan isn't just going to stand around and let God's people be blessed. Even though we went through a very difficult season, we learned that Christ never once abandoned us. See, that horrible battle we went through has caused my faith to grow. When I pray for someone, I expect to see miracles happen. When I lay hands on people, I don't just hope they will be set free, I really believe they are going to be set free.

God allows us to go through things to build our faith. The Word says that the thing that pleases God most about us is our faith. Hebrews 11:6 For many years I didn't realize this, but I do now. If we are in Christ, and Christ is in us, and Christ laid hands on the sick and they were healed, then why can't I do it, too? Jesus went about doing the Father's business. The Father wants all his children to be getting freed, blessed and healed. It amazes me how many Christians say "I want to know the Father's will." Well, just start doing the things that Christ did. So many Christians I know or have met are afraid to get into spiritual warfare or confront a witch.

I ask people. "How often do you read your Bible?" Jesus himself had to battle some very evil spirits. If we would run to the battle instead of waiting for the battle to come to us, I believe we would see more signs, wonders and miracles. Too many people don't realize the power they possess. It was the Holy Spirit working through Christ that set demon-possessed people free. It was the Holy Spirit working through Christ that raised the dead. It was the Holy Spirit in Christ that healed the broken-hearted. First John 4:4 says "He that is in you is greater than he that is in the world." Also in Romans 8:47, it states that we are *more* than conquerors.

Many times mediums come against ministries in séances and speak all kinds of lies, but there's one thing that the enemy can't stand against: It's a Christian that is under the blood of Christ. This is why we need to plead the blood of Christ daily over our children, our bank accounts, our cars, ourselves, yes, even our friends. Many times I have witnessed this happen in my own personal life. As I was engaged in heavy warfare, seducing spirits would go out and attacked people who were close to me. Then these people would come against me! They didn't realize that they were being used by the enemy to attack my character or my anointing.

Of all the evil spirits, I believe it is the seducing spirits that do more damage than others, because they are very sneaky and hide really well. I have seen people gossip that normally would never do that, but I could tell that a seducing spirit was really attacking a person and wanting that person to speak out against a ministry. I would not join with most Christians I have met to engage in spiritual warfare, because when the battle heats up, they start complaining than its an all-out war against them, because they have sinned, and they're giving Satan an open door to attack. So I find myself interceding for them too.

I have a good friend that I admire a lot, because he can't be shaken with fear or doubt. He is solid like a rock, and just loves people and wants everyone to be set free. I have met other men that had great faith, but he just smiles when the battle heats up. Many Christians have asked how it is that I did not get destroyed, or if I know people that got badly harmed when they engaged in spiritual warfare. Hosea 4:6 says that God's people are destroyed from a lack of knowledge. The people I know that ended up in bad shape by engaging in spiritual warfare were the ones who didn't take it very seriously. See, many Christians, especially those in leadership, don't realize that it is their faith that the enemy hates so much, because it's our faith that defeats the enemy. 1 John 5:4

Many years ago when I wore a pentagram, there were people who were afraid to stand by me in line at grocery stores or even sit by me in a church. I thought it was amazing how on a Sunday afternoon people would be at the grocery store talking about God. My heart just yearned to know Him, but most Christians were afraid of my satanic jewelry. By what I have witnessed myself, the Church is so weak at understanding the power they have that it doesn't surprise me when I hear about a church or a ministry being destroyed. See, my first pastor did something I would like to see more churches do. He had the teenagers do spiritual warfare. I have told many people that if you want to see signs and wonders, have teenagers who are radical for Christ do the praying. My greatest experiences of seeing miracles were when I have seen teenagers pray. A lot of teenagers I have met think the word "warfare" is cool. So they would dive in and there is nothing holding back their faith.

I believe the church has become so weak because we have watered down the Word so much that many Christians can't even agree on very simple things. I have even read reports of people wondering if Christ really did die on the cross, or if the Holy Spirit really does exist. This grieves me deeply, because it's Christ's blood that gives us the power to engage in spiritual warfare. It's the loving Holy Spirit that gives us the wisdom to know what's going on. Then he gives us the power to engage in spiritual warfare.

I praise God for my pastor, because he has been given a lot of wisdom on knowing how to pray for a person and just what to say when he talks to a person. One thing I admire about him is that he speaks the actual Word of God. He doesn't sugarcoat anything, and I deeply admire this, because I have seen so many pastors afraid to speak the straight truth. They sugarcoat what they have to say in so many ways. I have seen them compromise the Word to where I wondered what *do* they really mean to say.

Many times I have heard the Holy Spirit say, "When will the church humble itself and seek God's face? When will my people quit talking about yesterday's blessings and start living in the blessings of today?" See, God wants us to be praising Him daily for the great healings, breakthroughs, prosperity, and restoration that He is doing in the lives of people today! God wants us to see marriages restored, people set free, finances coming in and major breakthroughs happening on a regular basis.

I have seen people praising God for hours on Sundays because of all the miracles that are happening. Services like that can last four or five hours! I don't want just to hear about God's goodness years ago. I want to hear about what God is doing today! I want more of God in my life today, so I can brag more about how awesome He is. A man I know was talking about the how great the NFL playoffs were, but I said to him, "If you want to see something great, lay your hands on the sick and watch them be healed right before your eyes. Lay your hands on someone and prophesy over their lives, and realize they just got their confirmation."

Personally, I really enjoy praying, but when God gives me an opportunity to prophesy over someone's life, I really get excited with them, because we should never take a prophetic word lightly. People have said to me, "I want the power of God in my home or in my church but it doesn't seem to be there." If you really want to see the power of God flow in your home, get rid of everything that is openly against the Word of God. My wife and I can't expect God to flow freely in our home if we are glorifying sin on the TV set, or if we are glorifying sin on our computer. If you want God to flow freely in your home or your church, just invite the Holy Spirit to show you what you need to do. Let Him know he is welcome! He is so loving and gentle that his presence is exciting just to be around.

After a long day at work, I like to put on worship music. One day I asked the Holy Spirit to reveal to me why so many Christians could not help me. The spirit of God revealed to me that to really help someone who has been involved in so many demonic things, one must intercede on their behalf daily and meditate on God's Word daily. I personally believe in having worship music playing in my home all the time. Not what's on the radio, but true worship music.

True worship music is powerful, and when it's being performed, it does something to the inner man. Radio stations will play just what sounds good to the ears, but true worship music isn't just trying to sound good. It's more focused on what is pleasing to God Almighty. Most radio stations play music mainly to entertain and keep their audience.

Real worship music is all about God and His glory and power. I have met some worship leaders who usher in the presence of God, and others that just direct the music, and that's all. True worshippers will tell you that it's not about the words or the instruments. It's all about letting God know you love him. Real worship music ushers in the power of God to where demons cringe and eventually leave.

We once had a worship leader that just made you feel like God's presence was so thick that you couldn't help but fall in love with God. Whenever I meet true worshipers, I feel so blessed just to be around them, because they want the same thing I want, and that is, we want more of God.

When I was involved in the occult, I didn't ever get bothered when someone was playing Christian music downloaded from the radio, but when I heard a real worshiper sing, I would feel sick to my stomach. Real worship music carries a very powerful anointing, especially if it openly exalts Jesus Christ. When we truly worship the King of Kings, Lord of Lords, we can expect to see miracles, signs and wonders. I am going to go out on a limb here and say if your church isn't experiencing signs and wonders, you should really start praying about the worship leader, because he or she is the one that ushers God's presence into the service.

We, as Christians, need to get this deep down in our spirit. We serve the Creator of the universe. He has so much awesome power! He is mighty, all-powerful, all-knowing and all-loving. We don't realize this many times, because what's being preached is so often a weak, boring, dead gospel. That's why I pray that whoever reads this book will get excited about Jesus Christ. Stop focusing on life's issues and start doing the Father's business!

I now have a very loving spiritual father in my life, and he helps me a lot. But if I would have listened to pastors a long time ago, I would still be dead in my sin, because many pastors didn't agree with my leaving their church or seeking out answers elsewhere when I didn't believe their answers to my questions were right. You don't belong just to a pastor or a church. If you know in your heart there's more of God elsewhere, really pray about what God wants you to do. Don't allow a pastor to hold you back from doing God's will. But walk in humility, especially if you don't agree with your pastor.

Too many people go to their pastor full of pride and try to correct him and then end up falling on their face. My spiritual father is a college professor at a university and a very good friend. I may not always agree with him, but I deeply appreciate him, because he's looking out for my best interests. Too many pastors don't look out for people's best interest. They put their own fears on their congregation. People ask me, "What is a good pastor?" I tell them that a great pastor is not afraid to send people out to other places to work for the Lord, and he is not afraid to discuss what sin is from behind the pulpit. Too many Christians are lazy and compromise their time. We must repent and go after God with all we have. We must stop trying to please ourselves and start pleasing God.

I realize there are things in this book that may offend some people, but my purpose is not to please man. I want to please God! God wants to perform signs and wonders through His people, but fewseem willing to humble themselves enough to do what God asks them to do. I have heard Christians say "God wants me to do this or that, but it doesn't make sense!" That's the problem! I don't care how educated you are or aren't and neither does God! Look at the facts! Jesus fed five thousand people with only five loaves of bread and two fishes. Mark 8:17. Does that make sense?

My first pastor walked in the anointing of signs and wonders. One thing he taught me was that when people say you can't do something, that's when your faith should rise up and say, "I can't, but God can." Jesus asked his disciples, "Why do you reason among yourselves?" See, quit trying to figure out God, and just take Him at His Word.

I know of a lot of successful men and women of God who just took God at His Word. I have met other people who just had excuses of why they couldn't do what God was asking them to do. Remember that there was one man that when Jesus said to come and follow him, the man said, "First let me first go and bury my father." Jesus is sending us a strong message here. Either he is the most important thing in your life, or you're not worthy of him. Matthew 22:14 says that many are called but few are chosen. I have seen people try to serve money and God at the same time, but that's impossible, because either God is number one or He's nothing. I have been to a church that exalted those who had great wealth, and the Holy Spirit right away said, "It's too bad they don't know the Word." I said, "I don't understand." So the Holy Spirit showed me Luke 12:15 where it says that one's life does not consist in the abundance of the things he possesses.

True humility is looking at others and saying, "Where can I help?" But pride is all about self. Many times in life I battled with things for long periods of time. Then one day, the Spirit of God said, "You need to have a hiding place to go to where it's just you and God." Well, in this place, I started to worship God and let Him know how great He was. I immediately saw that I was being set free. Then one night my life was forever changed. I was taken up in to the third heaven, and I was running around free and rejoicing, playful-like and just loving on God. Then I heard Jesus Christ say, "If you will just believe, you can have this all the time."

The next day, I went into the hiding place again, just to worship God. To my amazement, I found myself being set free from tormenting spirits. I really believed I was going to have to battle them all my life, but these demonic spirits were leaving me for good! After that, I discovered that when a person goes to a secret place to worship God, his life can and will be transformed. Matthew 6:5-6 As time went on and I kept worshipping God, I saw chains falling off of me. Many people find their identity in what they do for a living, and I used to be guilty of this. But when I started to really seeking out God and worshipping Him, I found that I am valuable no matter what I do in life, because my worth comes from Jesus Christ.

Before I got saved, I really believed that God was mean and hateful. I would hear demons talk to me, saying wicked things about God and mocking God. As time went on, I would actually converse at times with them. Some Christians I have prayed for have told me that they were confused a lot. They didn't realize it, but they had opened up a satanic door to where demons were able to talk to them and confuse them. We need to be aware that there is a spirit of confusion just like a spirit of lust that likes to confuse people. 1 Corinthians 14:33 I can't say enough how important it is to read God's Word every day and pray every day. Most atheists I have met really don't know really anything about God, because the spirit of confusion and the spirit of anti-Christ has blinded their eyes from seeing any truth at all. Most atheists just know that a Christian hurt them, and that planted a seed of unforgiveness in their heart.

When I first came to Christ, many people prayed over me with no results. When a person has been in occultism, we need to bind all demonic strongholds in their mind before we can do much to help them. When a person believes a lie, a stronghold is created in that person's heart. Satan is a master-deceiver. He mimics God in every way. I know people who struggled financially and walked away from God, and all of a sudden they came into great wealth. We need to constantly watch and pray, because Satan wants everybody to serve him. He especially wants Christians to fall away from God and serve him. He is a master at disguise and a master of deception.

Satan has deceived people for thousands of years into believing that he is good and that God is evil. Some people claim that Satan actually cares about them. It's so heart-breaking when I hear this, because Satan cares nothing at all about people. All he wants to do is hurt God by taking more souls to hell. I have met Christians who speak things against Satan. However, in the Bible, it says that Michael the archangel didn't even speak a word against devil, but said "The Lord rebuke you." Jude 9 Too many Christians have got it in their head that the occult and Satanism is mere child's play, or that spiritual warfare is just a casual thing. I have met dozens of people who have been blinded by Satan in these matters, and it cost them a lot.

A woman I met a while back asked me to really pray for a certain couple, so I went ahead and stood in agreement with her that God would bring them to their knees to repent. The man was a deacon and very well-liked, but he left his wife for another man. We, as Christians, need to quit acting like children and realize that Satan really has come to kill, steal and destroy. I find it amazing how many people don't want to realize that Satan isn't a toy to play with and his demons are just as real as he is. If you give Satan a chance to destroy you, he will.

When I was a child, I was fascinated with death, and this in turn opened up many doors for demonic spirits to come into my life. Since I found death so interesting, I invited in spirits that were connected with death such as spirits of sorrow, depression, suicide, hopelessness and tragedy. What you meditate on is what will happen to you. That is why God said to meditate on His Word day and night.

Since I had opened the door for so many demonic spirits when I was very young, I needed to do a lot of spiritual warfare before I could really start serving God with all my heart. I had developed a whole nest of demonic strongholds. Because God's loving Holy Spirit is a counselor, I was able to be set free and healed of so many things. See, I don't take my freedom lightly. I was actually going insane.

If you're willing to humble yourself and walk in humility, God will heal you and restore you. One thing I found amazing about the Holy Spirit is that he is very patient and understanding. I had to walk to Christ with baby steps, and I was set free through taking baby steps. I have learned that when you open many doors to demonic powers, you can't just shut all of them at once, because certain doors that you have to walk through require a lot of forgiveness first, and then the door can easily be shut.

People have asked me what was my greatest experience was of the Holy Spirit exposing a lie that I had believed for a long time. I didn't realize how many lies I had believed about myself until the Holy Spirit spoke to me one day and said, "I am going to start exposing lies you believe to be the truth." Since I have gotten to know the Holy Spirit as God and a real being, I have realized that the Holy Spirit gets much more excited about our freedom in Christ than we do. I have witnessed the Holy Spirit get rid of so many strongholds in my mind that sometimes I have been literally transformed into being more like Christ within hours. One time I was having just a great day with the Holy Spirit, and he led me to 2 Samuel 5:20, where Baal perazim means "master of breakthrough". God is the master of breakthroughs. No matter if it's financial, spiritual, emotional, or physical, God Almighty can do it!

I have discovered that the more I praise God with my life, the more breakthroughs I have. I don't know a lot of people who have had to deal with tormenting spirits like I have, but I will tell you this: It's very difficult to believe anything when tormenting spirits refuse to give up. So when I was set free of all those tormenting spirits, it did so much for me that I was literally changed forever. One thing I can't emphasize enough is that if you're in need, go to the Father and ask Him for help. This whole book is about God's mercy and grace towards me.

I didn't do anything special. God just wants the message out everywhere. He loves sinners. My parents have always been very loving and supportive, but I saw their pain, because they knew I was in a lot of pain, but they didn't know how to help me. My parents spent thousands of dollars on me for rehabilitation programs, psychologists, therapists, and counselors. But God, the loving Father that He is, set me free for good!

I used to yearn to know what it would be like not to be severely depressed and bound by so many bizarre fears. I wanted to know what life would be like not meditating on suicide, but the thoughts of suicide just kept coming. I thought it was natural to think about death all the time.

After losing my brother, it was very difficult to deal with life. Whenever anyone would stop by that had children when I was young, their kids would play with my toys, and I would feel sick inside, because I would think of how my brother and I had played together. I wanted my brother back so badly to talk to. So many times I would go to my pretend coffin and pretend he was there beside me. I went through years of therapy trying to cope with my brother's death with no relief at all.

But as I began to really get to know Jesus Christ as my Savior, he began to restore me and take all that pain away. I am not saying that at times I don't miss my brother, because I will always miss him, but I am not bogged down in depression anymore because he's gone. As I have walked through this pain, I have had to learn to forgive a lot of people, and I have had to let go of all my resentments and bitterness towards God. It hasn't been easy, but I would not change a single thing that has happened, because knowing God the way I know Him is so much more valuable to me than all the tears I have shed.

Jesus Christ is so much more awesome than I could ever put into words, because his love and genuineness is so incredible that when you come to realize this, it will make you cry. People have asked me what caused me to change and not go into mental wards anymore. The answer is that when I got sick and tired of going nowhere in life, I finally asked God to take over my life.

If you really want God to help you and change you, you need to be totally honest and completely surrender to Him. This might surprise a lot of people, but I thought Satanism and witchcraft was really cool at first. I thought, "Wow, I have finally tapped into the most awesome power, and now I can be happy." But everything I did just took me farther away from what I really desired.

A friend of mine called me Natas at times, which is Satan spelled backwards. I thought, "Wow, this is cool!" Once a friend of mine and I were talking about Satanism really loudly in a grocery store, and we were scaring people really bad. So we ended up going to a restaurant, and we did the same thing there with the same results. Looking back, I feel so sorry for all those people because they didn't know about the power in the blood of Jesus.

Since getting saved, I have read many books about spiritual warfare, but hardly any helped me. A person with just a lot of head knowledge can't understand the battles I have had in my mind. I have come to realize that the Bible talks a lot about the power of praise. I can't say enough about this. Second Chronicles 20:21 points out how praise defeats the enemy. Ever since I had my eyes opened to real worship music, I enjoy having it around me all the time. If a demonic spirit tries to come attack you, put on real worship music, because the enemy doesn't like listening to really anointed music. I believe music should get us excited about wanting to know and serve God. Music wasn't created for us, it was created by us--to let God know how much we adore Him and love Him.

Conclusion

Many people are bound with hopelessness and discouragement, believing that there is no hope, or that God is the cause of their problems. So they live with a constant nagging going on inside them that there is no hope, so they should just give up; that life is meaningless.

For many years I would constantly hear those words in my spirit: God doesn't care about you. God doesn't love you. You're worthless and your life is worthless. Day and night I battled with these thoughts, wondering why I was even alive, that I couldn't do this or that, or that I was a complete failure at everything I did.

But I am now able to make the bold statement that Jesus Christ loves you right now and just the way you are. Many may say that the Church has done this or that to them, or that a pastor did this or that, or that a Christian leader or pastor didn't help out when they were most needed, or that they knew a Christian who did this or that.

All these circumstances are based upon human beings letting them down or hurting them. If this describes you, I am so deeply sorry that this happened to you, but please take it from me: Jesus Christ never let you down or abandoned you. He had nothing to do with your discouragement or confusion or hurt.

When I was in a psychiatric ward or a rehabilitation center, as I was so many times, many gave up on me. When I slit my wrist, things did look hopeless. When I was rejected multiple times by pastors of different churches, things really began to look hopeless. But that is just where when you need to say, "No, I refuse to accept all this doubt," or "I refuse to believe that a loving God will abandon me now."

I have been through a lot of rejection and hurt and pain, but none of it was or is God's fault in any way. A true Christian can either represent Christ Jesus or not represent him. God gave man a free will to do the right thing at all times, but many Christians walk in fear and ignorance, so please don't just take what you hear from others about God as being the whole truth. Get to know God, and you will see that He is filled with mercy, compassion, grace, understanding and love.

There is a big difference between knowing someone and knowing about someone. Many claim to know me and many claim how they have done this or that for me, but very few people truly know me.

Jesus Christ isn't just a figment of the imagination, a nice bedtime story, or just a man who lived a long time ago. He is and always will be the revelation of the living God, who is my dearest and closest friend, who has brought so much restoration to me and given me an abundance of blessings beyond anything I could ever imagine.

Someone reading this book could be like I was, a God-hater who saw Christ as just a fairy tale. But please let me point this out: Jesus Christ understands and feels your pain. It doesn't matter what your circumstances may be, there is hope in Christ if you will just cry out to him with a sincere heart. He will listen and he will be there for you, but you must do your part, which is to cry out to him from your heart of hearts, because he really does love you and doesn't want you to walk in all that hurt, anger, shame, resentment, bitterness, depression, fear, loneliness, grief and hopelessness any more. Romans 10:13

Many times i have felt that there was no use continuing to hang on to hope, but when there's no hope, that's just when Jesus Christ can come in even greater power, because with Christ, there is hope. In the Bible, 1Timothy 1:7 states that God has not given us a spirit of fear, but of love, power and a sound mind. If we meditate on what a sound mind is, we will quickly realize that a sound mind is one that thinks clearly, has healthy thoughts and healthy emotions. Jesus Christ died on the cross so that we can have this blessing, but with all blessings, we need to humble ourselves and cry out to Jesus Christ.

Thank you for taking the time to read this book. I really hope it has brought you encouragement and a deeper love for Jesus Christ. If this book has blessed you, I hope you will send me an email or a letter.

Be blessed!

<u>To Contact Tim Thompson send a letter to:</u>

Tim Thompson
8177 S. Harvard Ave,
Box 610 Tulsa,
OK, 74137

<u>Or Email him at:</u>

timthompson74@gmail.com

CPSIA information can be obtained at www.ICGtesting.com
Printed in the USA
LVOW08s0833190916

505148LV00030B/482/P